A High Schooler's Guide to Web Development

<Rithul Bhat/>

Rithul Bhat

A High Schooler's Guide to Web Development, First Edition

Copyright © 2025 by Rithul Bhat

To Ajja and Ajji

Thank you for your encouragement and wisdom

Preface

Ever since writing *A High Schooler's Guide to Java* in March of 2024, I've been thinking of other coding principles that would be helpful to the community. To help, I thought about myself and my coding journey. The first bit of coding (other than block coding) that I had ever done was HTML and CSS. These fundamentals were the building blocks of everything I had learned after, and it's worth noting their significance for programming in general.

Just like most programming languages, however, while there were many online resources and books to help learn these concepts, there was no clear and easy-to-understand method to actually learn.

This book is the solution to all those things - with structured chapters, checks for understanding, and a glossary at the end to check for keywords, this book is the perfect mini kickstarter to any web development you want to do, especially since it's written from a high schooler's perspective!

Like my last guide (Java), this book assumes you have no prior knowledge, giving step-by-step detailed explanations and fundamental overviews of HTML, CSS, and JavaScript (we'll go over these later). Feel free to jump from chapter to chapter, but note that a few projects may be built chronologically.

- Rithul Bhat

Table of Contents

- Margin & Padding
- Width & Height
- Fonts
- Tables
- Lists
- Forms
- Check For Understanding

- What is Bootstrap?
- Uses of Bootstrap
- Check For Understanding

- What is JavaScript?
- Where is JavaScript Used?
- First JavaScript Program
- The Script Tag
- Console.log()
- Variables and Data Types
- Functions
- Conditional Statements
- Loops
- Arrays
- Check for Understanding

- Variables

- Functions
- Interacting with HTML with IDs
- Check for Understanding

- Home.html
- AboutUs.html
- Contact.html

- HTML Terms
- CSS Terms
- JavaScript Terms

Chapter 1: How Should I Use This Book?

The first thing to understand while using this book is that it is made specifically for people who are attempting to break into website creation/development. Therefore, the book is centered around middle/high school basic HTML, CSS, and JavaScript topics and is structured as a beginner might see.

Use the **Glossary** at any point during the book if there is terminology you do not understand.

Structure To Remember

While reading through this book and learning new concepts, there is a **structure** that you should look out for in every chapter so that you know the purpose of the content that is being presented to you. The way the book is laid out is made so that it will create a structured learning path for you to fully grasp the concept you are learning! Take a look at the breakdown below:

1. Chapter header

2. Definition of concept in an easy-to-understand explanation

3. The various types of examples that fall under this concept and what these examples do

4. The examples

5. Check for understanding

When you read this book, have Visual Studio Code, or VS Code, (the place where you will type your code) open so you can keep up with the code and examples. We will set up VS Code in a few pages.

Chapter 2: Getting Started With Web Development

HTML Introduction

In short, HTML is a markup language. That's obvious – but what exactly do markup languages do? HTML, or HyperText Markup Language, is the foundation of every web page you see online. It structures content by using elements and tags to define headings, paragraphs, images, links, and much more.

First introduced in 1993, HTML has grown alongside the web, becoming an essential tool for web development. Without HTML, the internet as we know it wouldn't exist. HTML isn't just about writing code – it's about building the structure of websites and creating the blueprint that browsers such as Microsoft Edge or Google Chrome read to display content. From simple text to complex web applications, HTML is at the core of it all.

Whether you're crafting basic web pages or diving into advanced web development, learning HTML will not only help with school projects but will also lay the groundwork for future skills in web design, software engineering, and app development.

Before you start writing HTML or building websites, you'll need to set up a few things to ensure the best experience.

Where Do I Write My Code?

With most programming languages, you can either write your code in a terminal or an IDE (Integrated Development Environment). A terminal is a text-based software that can execute code directly on your computer. This is also known as PowerShell or console. If you go to your computer's "Search" bar, click on the terminal, and get a feel for what it is like.

While a terminal is a great way to code and practice, it is best to use an IDE when learning and testing new things out. An IDE, which stands for Integrated Development Environment, is basically an editor for all your code.

The first step to learning Web Development is to understand where and how to write your code, so it is time to install an IDE on your computer. There are several IDEs you can use, however, the most popular IDE for this kind of coding is Visual Studio Code, also known as VS Code.

While you may use other IDEs, it is highly recommended to use VS Code as it is free and easy to use. All the examples and run-throughs will be written on it.

If you already have an IDE installed, skip to the next chapter. If not, take a look below for download instructions.

How To Install Visual Studio Code

Read the following instructions to get your IDE set up on your computer.

1. Go to your default web browser (Chrome, Safari, Edge, etc) and search for "Visual Studio Code Download".

2. Click on the link that says "Download Visual Studio Code". It should be the first link. If you cannot find it, type the link below in the search bar: "https://code.visualstudio.com/download"

It should look something like this:

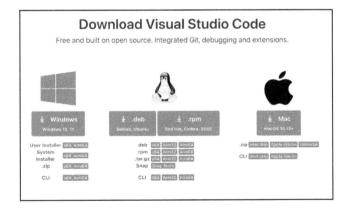

3. Click on the Download button. There should be 3 or 4 available for you to choose from. Simply click on the button for your operating system. Then, open the download in your file directory (or Finder) and then follow the steps to get it installed successfully on your computer.

4. If done properly, you should be able to open VS Code as any other app on your computer, leading to this page. If you see this, you are all set!

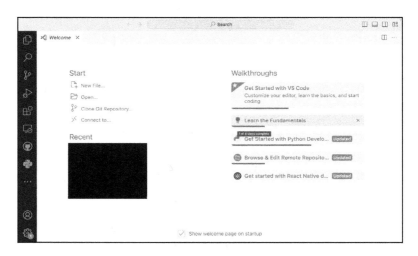

VS Code Basics

Now that your IDE is set up and your computer is updated, it is important to understand how to properly use it so that you can have the best learning experience!

Upon entering the app, you should see the welcome screen.

Let's write our first simple program.

First HTML Program

Now that Visual Studio Code (VS Code) is set up and ready to go, it's time to write your first HTML program! Follow this step-by-step guide to create a basic web page:

1. **Open VS Code**
2. **Create a New File**
   - In the navigation bar (navbar) at the top of your screen, click on "File"
   - Now, click on the option of "New File"
3. **Name Your File**
   - Type in the name in the pop-up window. Let's name it "helloWorld.html"
4. **Save Your File in a Folder**
   - Create a folder in your file directory called "Web Development". You can name this folder whatever you'd like.

○ Follow the prompts to save the file in that folder

I will use the "Web Development" folder to hold all our files for this book.

Later, when you want to open that file back up, you can click "Open Folder" and click on that folder!

3. Set Up Basic HTML Structure.

Inside helloWorld.html, type ! and hit **Enter**. VS Code will automatically generate a basic HTML5 template for you.

4. Press **Ctrl + S** (or **Cmd + S** on Mac) to save your file. Always make it good practice to do this after adding in some code.

5. Write some code!

Now, add the following code in between the two pieces of text that read <body>:

```
<h1> Hello World </h1>
```

Your code and IDE should look something like this:

```
1   <!DOCTYPE html>
2   <html lang="en">
3   <head>
4       <meta charset="UTF-8">
5       <meta name="viewport" content="width=device-width, initial-scale=1.0">
6       <title>Document</title>
7   </head>
8   <body>
9       <h1> Hello World </h1>
10  </body>
11  </html>
```

READ CAREFULLY: This entire book, you MUST save your code (ctrl + s) before running it. This is the only way you will see any changes when you refresh your browser!!

6. Open Your HTML File in a Browser.

Navigate to your File Explorer or Finder, and find the helloWorld.html file that you are currently working with. Then, right-click on that file and select "Open With" and then the browser of your choice. I will select Chrome.

7. View Your Page.

If you did the previous step, a new browser tab will open, displaying your "Hello World!" message.

8. Celebrate Your First web page!

Congratulations! You've created and run your first HTML program. This simple page is the foundation for much more complex and interactive websites you'll build in the future.

Chapter 3: HTML Overview

What is HTML?

HTML, or HyperText Markup Language, is the standard language used to create and design web pages. It provides the basic structure for all web content, organizing elements like text, images, and links into a readable format for web browsers.

Key Points:

- HTML is not a programming language; it's a markup language.
- It uses tags to define and format content.
- HTML is the first layer of any web page, often combined with CSS (for styling) and JavaScript (for interactivity).

HTML Setup File

Before we start building web pages, let's set up the necessary environment (most of this should be done by now):

1. Install Visual Studio Code (VS Code):
   o Download and install VS Code from https://code.visualstudio.com.
2. Create a New HTML File:
   o Open VS Code and select File → New File.

- Let's create a new file called text.html and hit enter
3. Set Up Basic HTML:
    - Inside the text.html file, type ! and press **Enter** and Save the file by **Ctrl + S** (or **Cmd + S** on Mac)
    - VS Code will generate a basic HTML template. This is the starting point for every web page.

Page Structure

Let's break down the default HTML5 structure. Look at the code snippet below or the code from your First Program to reference these explanations.

1. <!DOCTYPE html> – Document Type Declaration

- This is the very first line in any HTML5 document.
- It tells the browser to use the latest version of HTML (HTML5).
- Without this line, the browser may switch to quirks mode, potentially causing display issues.
- Think of it as the browser's cue to treat the document as modern HTML.

2. <html lang="en"> – Root HTML Tag

- The <html> tag wraps the entire HTML document. It signals the start of the web page.
- The lang="en" attribute specifies the language of the document (English in this case). This helps with accessibility and SEO (Search Engine Optimization).
- The closing tag </html> marks the end of the HTML document.

3. <head> – Head Section (Metadata)

- The <head> contains information about the page that isn't directly visible to users.
- Metadata helps define the character set, viewport settings, and title of the web page.

4. <body> – Body Section (Visible Content)

- The <body> contains everything users will see and interact with on the web page – text, images, buttons, and more.
- This is the core of the web page's visual and interactive elements.

This content is mainly for generic understanding - you do not need to completely understand it now. Intermittently come back to this section and you should understand it completely by the end of the book!

Check For Understanding

1. What does HTML stand for?

2. Which tag defines the visible part of an HTML document?

3. What is the purpose of the <h1> tag?

4. Why is the <!DOCTYPE html> declaration important?

By the end of this chapter, you should feel comfortable setting up an HTML file and understanding the basic structure of a web page.

Check For Understanding (Answers)

1. HyperText Markup Language

2. <body>

3. Creates a header of the largest size

4. Tells the browser to use HTML5

Chapter 4: Text in HTML

Introduction to Text

Text is one of the most fundamental elements of any web page. HTML provides a variety of ways to display, organize, and format text, allowing you to create everything from simple paragraphs to large headings and bold statements.

In this chapter, we'll cover how to:

- Display basic text on a web page.
- Use different text elements like headings and paragraphs.
- Format text for emphasis and readability.

Tags in HTML

Tags are the fundamental building blocks of HTML, defining the structure and content of a web page. An HTML tag consists of an opening tag, content, and a closing tag. They are usually between "<" and ">". For example, in

```
<h1> This is a header. </h1>
```

<h1> is the opening tag and </h1> is the closing tag. Notice how the closing tag has a slash in it while the opening does not. Tags help browsers understand how to display different elements, such as headings, paragraphs, images, and links.

The good thing about IDEs is that they usually autocomplete these ending tags for you once you type the opening tag, which saves time and effort on your part.

Display Text

Now, it is time to use specific tags within our code to print text according to our preferences. Tags are the code in between the "<" and ">" symbols, which you notice on the body and html tags. They define what our program ultimately looks like.

Printing text in HTML is straightforward. You simply use tags like <p> or <h1> and write your content between them.

Exploring Heading Tags (h1 - h6)

As you begin experimenting with HTML, you will notice that heading tags range from <h1> to <h6>, with <h1> being the largest and <h6> the smallest.

These headings help structure content, making web pages easier to read and navigate.

Headers follow the following syntax:

```
<h[#]> Header Text </h[#]>
```

Basically, we choose what size header we want in our tag, and then place what the header says in between the two tags.

Now, modify your **text.html** (from the previous chapter) file by typing all heading tags within the <body> tag:

```
<h1>Look at this H1 heading</h1>
<h2>Look at this H2 heading</h2>
<h3>Look at this H3 heading</h3>
<h4>Look at this H4 heading</h4>
<h5>Look at this H5 heading</h5>
<h6>Look at this H6 heading</h6>
```

Save the file text.html (ctrl + s) and refresh (ctrl + r) your browser to view the web page. You'll see that each heading gets progressively smaller.

The Paragraph Tag (<p>)

HTML paragraphs are created using the <p> tag. This tag allows you to separate blocks of text, improving readability and organization on your web page.

Each paragraph tag starts a new line and adds space above and below the text by default.

Paragraphs help structure content into digestible sections, which enhances user experience. Without paragraphs, text would appear as one long block, making it difficult to read.

Kind of like header tags, a p tag has around the same syntax:

```
<p> Paragraph text </p>
```

Add the following to your **text.html** file:

```
<p>This is a paragraph! </p>
```

Save your file and refresh your browser to see how paragraphs are displayed. You'll notice that our <p> tag is smaller than our <h6>!

Experiment and Observe

Try modifying the text inside the tags and adding new ones. Change the heading sizes, add more text in the paragraphs, and see how your page updates. This will help you understand how HTML organizes content visually.

Line Breaks

Sometimes you may want to break a line without starting a new paragraph. The <br> tag is used to insert a single line break. Unlike the <p> tag, it does not create spacing above or below the text; it simply moves the content after it to the next line.

Type this code into your text.html file:

```
<br>
```

Line breaks are particularly useful for displaying addresses, poetry, or any content that requires distinct lines but is part of the same block. Adding two <br> can make an extra line in between if you'd like that as well.

On top of all that, it is a super simple tag!

Formatting Text

HTML allows you to apply formatting to text to create emphasis, highlight important information, or improve readability. The following tags are commonly used for text formatting:

- Bold Text: <strong> or <b>
- Italic Text: <em> or <i>
- Underline Text: <u>
- Strikethrough Text: <s>

Try this in your code and see how it changes the look of your page. I would suggest adding new tags instead of manipulating old ones, therefore allowing you to see the changes taking place more easily.

You'll start to see a common pattern between the tags and how we display information in HTML, just look at this syntax for bold, italics, underline and strikethrough text:

```
<b> Bolded Text </b>
<i> Italicized Text </i>
<u> Underlined Text </u>
<s> Strikethrough Text </s>
```

I added the following examples for their respective formatting. Type this into **text.html**:

Bold:

```
<p><b>This entire paragraph is
bold.</b></p>
<p>This sentence has <b>some bold
text</b> in the middle.</p>
```

Italics:

```
<p><i>This entire paragraph is
italicized.</i></p>
<p>This sentence has <i>some italic
text</i> in the middle.</p>
```

Underline:

```
<p><u>This entire paragraph is
underlined.</u></p>
<p>This sentence has <u>some underlined
text</u> in the middle.</p>
```

Strikethrough:

```
<p><s>This entire paragraph is
strikethrough.</s></p>
<p>This sentence has <s>some
strikethrough text</s> in the
middle.</p>
```

This is what the final code looks like for this chapter, and the resulting web page as well:

```
text.html   ×                                                                    [] ..
text.html > html > body > p
 1   <!DOCTYPE html>
 2   <html lang="en">
 3   <head>
 4       <meta charset="UTF-8">
 5       <meta name="viewport" content="width=device-width, initial-scale=1.0">
 6       <title>Hello World!</title>
 7   </head>
 8   <body>
 9       <h1>Look at this H1 heading</h1>
10       <h2>Look at this H2 heading</h2>
11       <h3>Look at this H3 heading</h3>
12       <h4>Look at this H4 heading</h4>
13       <h5>Look at this H5 heading</h5>
14       <h6>Look at this H6 heading</h6>
15
16
17       <p>This is a paragraph!</p>
18
19       <br>
20
21       <p><b>This entire paragraph is bold.</b></p>
```

```
22      <p>This sentence has <b>some bold text</b> in the middle.</p>
23
24      <p><i>This entire paragraph is italicized.</i></p>
25      <p>This sentence has <i>some italic text</i> in the middle.</p>
26
27      <p><u>This entire paragraph is underlined.</u></p>
28      <p>This sentence has <u>some underlined text</u> in the middle.</p>
29
30      <p><s>This entire paragraph is strikethrough.</s></p>
31      <p>This sentence has <s>some strikethrough text</s> in the middle.</p>
32
33
34
35  </body>
36  </html>
```

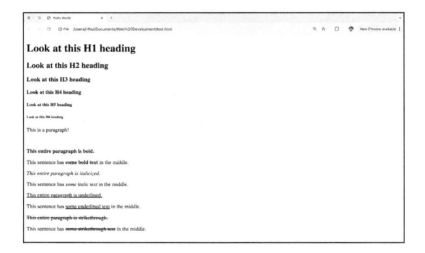

Check For Understanding

1. Which tag is used to define a paragraph in HTML?

2. How many levels of headings are available in HTML?

3. What tag creates bold text?

4. How do you insert a line break in HTML?

5. Which tag is used to italicize text?

Check For Understanding (Answers)

1. <p>

2. Six (from <h1> to <h6>)

3. <strong> or <b>

4.

5. <em> or <i>

Chapter 5: Elements & Attributes

Introduction to Elements & Attributes

In the previous chapter, we learned about basic text elements like headings and paragraphs. These elements are the building blocks of your web pages. Now, we'll dive deeper into the concept of HTML elements and introduce a crucial aspect: attributes. Let's create a new HTML file for this chapter called **elements.html**. Type the "!" for your setup as usual.

What Is An Element?

An **element** in HTML is essentially a single component of your web page. It's defined by opening and closing tags, like <p> for a paragraph or <h1> for a heading.

- **Opening tag:** Begins with a less than symbol (<) and ends with a greater than symbol (>).
- **Closing tag:** Similar to the opening tag, but includes a forward slash (/) before the element name.

For example:

- <p> is the opening tag for a paragraph.
- </p> is the closing tag for a paragraph.

The content that you want to appear on your web page goes between the opening and closing tags.

What Is An Attribute?

Attributes provide additional information or instructions for an HTML element. They are written within the opening tag, separated from the element name by a space.

The syntax for an attribute looks as follows:

```
<opening tag elementName
attribute="value"> </tag>
```

Here's an example. Type this into the <body> tag of **elements.html**:

```
<h1 style="color:blue;"> This is blue
</h1>
```

Throughout this chapter, we will learn several examples of elements and attributes working together in HTML.

Style Attribute

The style attribute allows you to apply styles directly to an element. This can be useful for quick styling adjustments.

Look at the syntax for the style attribute:

```
<elementname style="property: value;">
```

Add the following code to **elements.html** to see the changes!

```
<p style="color: blue; font-size:
48px;">This paragraph is blue and
larger.</p>
```

This paragraph will be displayed in blue and with a font size of 48 pixels Make sure to **save your code** and then **refresh your browser** to see these changes!

Images

The <img> element is used to display images on your web page. The most important attribute for the <img> element is src, which specifies the path to the image file. The syntax looks like this:

```
<img src="Image Path">
```

src attribute: This is the most crucial attribute. It specifies the path to the image file. The path can be relative (e.g., images/myimage.jpg) or absolute (e.g., https://www.example.com/image.jpg).

In order to get the image into your VSCode, just download a picture from online and save it in your "Web Development" folder.

Now, right-click on the image and rename it to "download"

My image's extension is "jpg" so my code will look as follows. Change your source path accordingly:

```
<img src="download.jpg">
```

I'll also add a break tag (<br>) after this line to clean up my web page for future elements. Save your code and refresh your page to see the changes.

Buttons

The <button> element creates interactive buttons on your web page, enabling user interaction.

Syntax:

```
<button>"Button text"</button>
```

Type the following code into your elements.html file:

Example (type in elements.html):

```
<button>Click Me!</button>
```

This simple code will create a button with the text "Click Me!". I want my next content to show up on the next line, so I will add a <br> tag after my button tag.

Adding Functionality:

To make the button act (like submitting a form), you'll typically use JavaScript. We'll explore JavaScript in detail in later chapters.

Linking

The <a> element (short for "anchor") is the cornerstone of web navigation. It allows you to create links to other web pages, files, or specific locations within the same page.

Syntax:

```
<a href="url">Display Text</a>
```

Example (type in elements.html):

```
<a href="https://www.google.com">Google</a>
```

href attribute: This is the most important attribute. It specifies the URL (Uniform Resource Locator) of the link.

The URL can be an external website (e.g., https://www.example.com) or an internal page within your website (e.g.)

Here, I'll also add another <br> tag after my link to space out my elements nicely. Here is what my code and web page look like right now:

```
elements.html
elements.html > html
1   <!DOCTYPE html>
2   <html lang="en">
3   <head>
4       <meta charset="UTF-8">
5       <meta name="viewport" content="width=device-width, initial-scale=1.0">
6       <title>Document</title>
7       <!--<link rel="stylesheet" href="styles.css">-->
8   </head>
9   <body>
10      <h1 style="color: blue;"> This is blue </h1>
11      <p style="color: blue; font-size: 48px;">This paragraph is blue and larger.</p>
12      <img src="download.jpg">
13      <br>
14      <button>Click Me!</button>
15      <br>
16      <a href="https://www.google.com">Google</a>
17  </body>
18  </html>
```

Tables

The <table> element is used to organize data in a structured format, making it easier to read and compare information.

Basic Structure:

- **<table>:** The main container for the table.
- **<tr>:** Defines a table row.
- **<th>:** Defines a table header cell (usually displayed bold or in a different font).
- **<td>:** Defines a table data cell.

Syntax:

```
<table>
    <tr>
        <th> </th>
        <th> </th>
    </tr>
    <tr>
        <th> </th>
        <th> </th>
    </tr>
</table>
```

Example (type in elements.html):

```
<table>
    <tr>
        <th>State</th>
        <th>Capital</th>
    </tr>
    <tr>
        <td>Texas</td>
        <td>Austin</td>
    </tr>
    <tr>
        <td>Missouri</td>
        <td>Jefferson City</td>
    </tr>
</table>
```

Refresh the page now. We don't really see the grid of the table, but we can see the generic layout.

You can edit the rows and columns depending on the information you want. If you utilize the "border" attribute, then you can see the grid of your table.

Add the following attribute to your <table> tag:

```
style="border: 1px solid black;
border-collapse: collapse;"
```

It should look like this:
```
<table style="border: 1px solid black;
border-collapse: collapse;">
```

Add the following attribute to each of your "th" and "td" tags:

```
style="border: 1px solid black;"
```

Here's an example of what a <th> and <td> tag should look like:

```
<th style="border: 1px solid
black;">State</th>
```

```
<td style="border: 1px solid
black;">Texas</td>
```

You should now see the grid around your table! Tables are especially helpful when you try to organize information, but also clever to use if you are trying to align multiple elements in a web page.

Lists

HTML offers two types of lists to present information in a clear and organized manner:

Unordered Lists (<ul>):

- Create a list of items with bullet points.
- Each list item is defined by the <li> tag.

Syntax:

```
<ul>
    <li> Item 1 </li>
    <li> Item 2 </li>
</ul>
```

Example (type in elements.html):

```
<ul id="groceryList">
    <li> Potatoes </li>
    <li> Tomatoes </li>
</ul>
```

Ordered Lists (<ol>):

- Create a numbered list.
- Each list item is also defined by the <li> tag.

Syntax:

```
<ol>
    <li> Item 1 </li>
    <li> Item 2 </li>
</ol>
```

Example (type in elements.html):

```
<ol id="bakingOrder">
    <li> Preheat oven. </li>
    <li> Whip batter. </li>
</ol>
```

Note: These are simplified explanations. You can explore more advanced table and list features, such as nested lists, table attributes (like border, width, cellspacing). We will go through most of the attributes in the later CSS chapter.

HTML Entities: Escaping Special Characters

In HTML, certain characters have special meanings. For example, the less than sign (<) and greater than sign (>) are used to delimit tags (e.g., <p>, </p>).

If you want to display these characters literally within your HTML content, you cannot simply type them directly. Doing so would likely cause the browser to misinterpret them as the beginning or end of a tag, leading to unexpected results.

To overcome this, HTML uses a system called entities. Entities are special codes that represent characters that are difficult or impossible to type directly in HTML. These entities begin with an ampersand (&) and end with a semicolon (;).

Here are some common HTML entities:

- Less than sign: <
- Greater than sign: >
- Ampersand: &
- Double quote: "
- Copyright symbol: ©
- Trademark symbol: ™
- Registered trademark symbol: ®

Example (type in elements.html):

```
<p> This is a (&gt;) symbol</p>
```

Common Attributes:

In addition to the other attributes we learned about, there

are a few commonly used attributes that will be used more than the others you have learned.

id: Assigns a unique identifier to an element, allowing you to target it with CSS or JavaScript (will learn in a later chapter).

Syntax:

```
<tag id= "ID Name"> </closing tag>
```

Example (type in elements.html):

```
<h1 id= "mainHeader"> This has the
mainHeader ID </h1>
```

class: Assigns one or more class names to an element, enabling you to style multiple elements with the same class using CSS.

Syntax:

```
<tag class= "Class Name"> This has a
Class Assigned to it </closing tag>
```

Example (type in elements.html):

```
<p class = "text" > I like coding </h1>
```

Other Stylistic Attributes: align attribute (for images): Controls the horizontal alignment of an image (e.g., align="left", align="right")

Example (type in elements.html):

```
<h3 style="text-align:
left;">left-aligned text</h3>
```

READ CAREFULLY: In the last 3 examples, you should've only seen a difference in the last (h3). ID and Class are core concepts you should know before CSS, but they won't change anything right now!

Comments in HTML

Comments are essential for writing clean, organized, and maintainable code. They allow developers to leave notes or explanations within the code without affecting how the web page functions.

Comments are ignored by the browser and are useful for documenting sections of code, debugging, or temporarily disabling certain elements during development. This means they do not affect the performance of your program as a whole.

In **HTML**, comments are written using <!-- -->:

After adding all of the examples from this chapter, your file should look something like this:

```html
elements.html  ×

1   <!DOCTYPE html>
2   <html lang="en">
3   <head>
4       <meta charset="UTF-8">
5       <meta name="viewport" content="width=device-width, initial-scale=1.0">
6       <title>Document</title>
7       <!--<link rel="stylesheet" href="styles.css">-->
8   </head>
9   <body>
10      <h1 style="color: █blue;"> This is blue </h1>
11      <p style="color: █blue; font-size: 48px;">This paragraph is blue and larger.</p>
12      <img src="download.jpg">
13      <br>
14      <button>Click Me:</button>
15      <br>
16      <a href="https://www.google.com">Google</a>
17      <br>
18
19      <!-- Continuing with tables and lists -->
20
21      <table style="border: 1px solid █black; border-collapse: collapse;">
```

```
22        <tr>
23            <th style="border: 1px solid ■black;">State</th>
24            <th style="border: 1px solid ■black;">Capital</th>
25        </tr>
26        <tr>
27            <td style="border: 1px solid ■black;">Texas</td>
28            <td style="border: 1px solid ■black;">Austin</td>
29        </tr>
30        <tr>
31            <td style="border: 1px solid ■black;">Missouri</td>
32            <td style="border: 1px solid ■black;">Jefferson City</td>
33        </tr>
34    </table>
35
36    <ul id="groceryList">
37        <li> Potatoes </li>
38        <li> Tomatoes </li>
39    </ul>
40
41    <ol id="bakingOrder">
42        <li> Preheat oven. </li>
43        <li> Whip batter. </li>
44    </ol>
45    |
46    <p> This is a (&gt;) symbol</p>
47
48    <!-- Common Attributes Examples-->
49
50    <h1 id= "mainHeader"> This has the mainHeader ID </h1>
51    <p class = "text" > I like coding </h1>
52    <h3 style="text-align: left;">left-aligned text</h3>
53 </body>
54 </html>
```

Check For Understanding

1. What does the "style" attribute do?

2. How do you represent the less than sign (<) in HTML?

3. How do you write a comment in HTML?

4. What are the opening and closing tags for the two types of lists we learned?

5. What is the attribute in an <a> tag that holds the actual url or filepath to whatever you are linking to?

6. Write the code for a button with the text "I like buttons"

7. Write a header of any size, with an ID of "header" and a value of "This is a header"

8. What are the 3 common tags you will find within the <table> tag?

Check for Understanding (Answers)

1. This attribute can add CSS styles within the HTML element.
2. <
3. `<!-- This is a comment -->`
4. Unordered List: <ul></ul>, Ordered List: <ol></ol>
5. href
6. `<button> I like buttons </button>`
7. `<h1 id="header"> This is a header </h1>`
8. `<tr>`, `<td>`, and `<th>`

Chapter 6: CSS Overview

What is CSS?

CSS, or Cascading Style Sheets, is a stylesheet language used to describe the presentation of an HTML document. While HTML is responsible for the structure and content of a web page, CSS controls how that content looks – including colors, fonts, spacing, and layout.

By separating content (HTML) from presentation (CSS), web developers can create visually appealing websites that are easier to maintain and update.

How CSS Helps Us

CSS is essential for web design for several reasons:

Consistency: CSS allows developers to apply the same style across multiple pages, ensuring a uniform look and feel.

Efficiency: One CSS file can control the appearance of an entire site, reducing redundancy.

Flexibility: You can easily make changes to your site's design by modifying the CSS file without altering the HTML structure.

User Experience: CSS can improve navigation, readability, and overall aesthetics, enhancing the user's experience.

Responsive Design: CSS enables websites to adapt to different screen sizes and devices.

Setting up our HTML & CSS Files

1. First, let's create our HTML page. Let's name it **index.html** and type ! on the first line and hit "Enter" to generate a basic HTML template for you. This is the same step that you learned in previous chapters.
2. Next, the same way you create an HTML page (File -> New File), let's make a CSS page called styles.css. Save both index.html and styles.css and it should be in your "Web Development" folder.

After the two files have been created, we have to link the two files together so that the HTML knows to use the CSS files when it creates the web page.

So, let's link them together. In between our two <head> tags in index.html, let's add the following code (after the <title> tag):

```
<link rel="stylesheet"
href="styles.css">
```

This creates a link of type stylesheet, with the name styles.css. Now, whenever we write CSS through the other file, it'll display on the html screen from index.html.

```
index.html ×
index.html
1    <!DOCTYPE html>
2    <html lang="en">
3        <head>
4            <meta charset="UTF-8">
5            <meta name="viewport" content="width=device-width, initial-scale=1.0">
6            <title>Document</title>
7            <link rel="stylesheet" href="styles.css">
8        </head>
9        <body>
10
11        </body>
12   </html>
```

Let's see this connection in action now. Type in the following HTML code in **index.html** for a welcome message.

```
<h1> Welcome to my CSS Website! </h1>
```

Save your code and open the browser! It should look plain as it did before.

Let's make it a bit nicer now. Head into your styles.css file and type in the following code and save the file. I will explain what it means in the next chapter.

```
h1 {
    text-align:center;
}
```

Now, refresh the browser. The text should be aligned in the center! This establishes our connection and shows how our CSS file affects our web page.

We just successfully completed an exercise of external CSS. Unlike the previous chapter, we style our page through another file outside of HTML.

Reasons we use CSS externally:

- **Clean Code:** Separating CSS from HTML keeps the code organized and easier to manage.

- **Reusability:** The same CSS file can be linked to multiple HTML files, ensuring consistency.
- **Scalability:** As your project grows, managing styles in a single CSS file simplifies future updates.

Check For Understanding

1. What does CSS stand for?

2. Why do we use an external CSS file instead of inline styling?

3. How do you link a CSS file to an HTML document?

4. Which CSS property changes the background color of a web page?

5. What tag is used to add a link to a CSS file inside the HTML document?

Check For Understanding (Answers)

1. Cascading Style Sheets

2. To keep HTML clean, reusable, and easier to manage

3. <link rel="stylesheet" href="css/style.css">

4. background-color

5. <link>

Chapter 7: CSS Usage

Throughout this chapter, I will give examples of what to add to our HTML file as well as CSS file. Try your best to follow along, putting the right code in the right file.

This chapter, we will build off of the index.html and styles.css file that we created in Chapter 6.

CSS Syntax

CSS syntax consists of selectors and declaration blocks. Take a look at the following syntax.

```
selector { property: value; }
```

Selectors identify the HTML elements you want to style, while declaration blocks contain the style rules enclosed in curly braces {}. Each rule comprises a property and a value, separated by a colon.

- Selector: Targets the HTML element (e.g., h1, p, .class, #id).
- Property: The style attribute (e.g., color, font-size).
- Value: Defines how the property is applied (e.g., blue, 16px).

Let's take a look into what we already wrote in our CSS file from the last chapter. When we see:

```
h1 {
    text-align: center;
}
```

It is pretty easy to break up h1 as the selector, text-align as the property, and center as the value. This means that every single h1 tag will be aligned to the center. However, there are several selectors, properties, and values that we will use to style elements!

What is a Class?

A class is a reusable attribute that can be applied to multiple elements. It allows you to style groups of elements the same way.

HTML Example:

Open the index.html file and add the following code:

```
<p class="intro">Welcome to the
website!</p>
<p class="intro">Let's learn CSS!</p>
```

CSS Class Syntax:

```
.className {
    property: value;
}
```

CSS Example:

Open the style.css file and add the following code:

```
.intro {
    text-align: right;
    font-size: 20px;
}
```

.intro is a class selector in CSS. Notice that we put a period before the class name in the CSS file.

Let's refresh your browser with our HTML file now. Instead of our small, left-aligned font that we usually see, we now see a bigger, right-aligned font instead.

Since we used the .intro selector, all elements with the intro class will be right-aligned and 20px big. You can play around with this, changing the size and other factors of the element to see how it is manipulated when you refresh it.

What is an ID?

An ID is like a class, but it is not reusable, and it is only for one single element in your web page.

HTML Example (type in index.html):

```
<p id="welcome">Here, we use an ID to
style text!</p>
```

CSS ID Syntax:

```
#idName {
    property: value;
}
```

CSS example (type in style.css):

```
#welcome {
    color: blue;
    font-size: 60px;
}
```

Refresh your browser! You should see a big blue "Hello!" printed on your screen. Remember, IDs are like classes except they can only be used once.

#welcome is an ID selector in CSS. Notice that we put a hashtag before the ID name in the CSS file. Therefore, the element with ID welcome will be blue with a size of 60 pixels.

Use ID (#) when:

- You have a unique element on the page that won't be repeated.
- You need to target a specific element for JavaScript.
- You want a higher specificity than a class.

Use Class (.) when:

- You need to reuse styles across multiple elements.
- You want to follow best practices for maintainability and flexibility.
- You want to apply multiple classes to a single element.

Refresh your browser! Look at all the stylistic changes occurring and think about what you could do in the future as well!

Colors

Color is one of the most essential aspects of CSS. It can transform a plain website into a visually appealing and engaging experience. CSS allows you to apply color to text, backgrounds, borders, and other elements by using various properties.

Applying Colors

- Text Color: The color property changes the color of the text.
- Background Color: The background color property sets the color behind the content.
- Border Color: The border-color property defines the color of element borders.

CSS Color Values:

Colors can be specified various ways, such as:

- Named Colors: Predefined colors like red, blue, green.
- Hex Codes: Represent colors using a six-digit code (e.g., #ff5733).
- RGB Values: Specify the intensity of red, green, and blue (e.g., rgb(255, 87, 51)). The range of each RGB value is anywhere from 0 to 255, inclusive.

RGBA Values: Same as RGB but with transparency/opacity as an option

Modify index.html and and add the following code:

```
<h1>CSS Colors</h1>

<p>CSS lets you apply vibrant colors to
web elements.</p>

<p class="highlight">This paragraph has
a highlighted background.</p>
```

Open the style.css file and add the following code:

```css
h1
{
    text-align: center;
    color: #ff6347;
}

body
{
    background-color: #f0f8ff;
}

p
{
    color: rgb(50, 50, 50);
}

.highlight {
    background-color: yellow;
    color: black;
}
```

From this CSS code, we can already predict that all h1 tags are centered and reddish-colored. The entire web page (the body tag) should be light blueish. All the p tags should be greyish (50, 50, 50). Finally, any element with the highlight class should have a yellow background color with black text.

You should be able to see the color changes within your web page! Notice how the style from a class will override styles from generic tag selectors like "p" in CSS.

For example, if we look at the p tag with a class of "highlight" the CSS will first take the styling from .highlight before the styling from the generic p selector! Here is a quick check of what you should see as of now:

Borders

Borders add structure and definition to HTML elements. The border property in CSS allows you to create lines around elements, making them stand out or separate from other sections.

Border Properties

- border-width: Sets the thickness of the border (e.g., 1px, 5px, etc).
- border-style: Defines the style (e.g., solid, dashed, dotted).
- border-color: Specifies the color of the border.

Update index.html to include a div:

```
<div class="box">
    This box has a dashed green border.
</div>
```

Syntax for border property:

```
border: width style color;
```

CSS example to give this div a border (type in style.css):

```
.box {
    border: 3px dashed #4caf50;
    background-color: #fff3cd;
}
```

Save your files and refresh your browser now to see the changes!

Feel free to play with other properties such as border-radius to notice the UI changes.

Margin & Padding

Margins and padding control the spacing around elements. While margin deals with space **outside** the element, padding manages space **inside** the element, between the content and the border.

Let's add on a few properties to the box class we had earlier:

```
.box {
    border: 3px dashed #4caf50;
    background-color: #fff3cd;
    padding: 10px;
    margin: 20px;
}
```

Refresh your browser to appropriately view these changes in spacing. If it doesn't seem as noticeable, make drastic changes and see what it looks like!

Width & Height

Width and height properties control the size of HTML elements.

Why Use Width and Height?

- **Control Layout:** Width and height let you organize elements, ensuring they align properly within a page.
- **Consistency:** Standardizing element sizes creates uniformity across your design.
- **Responsiveness:** Combined with relative units (%, vw, vh), elements can scale depending on the screen size.

Fixed vs. Fluid Sizes

- **Fixed Sizes** (px): Elements stay the same size regardless of screen size.
- **Fluid Sizes** (%, vw, vh): Elements adjust dynamically based on the screen or parent container size.

Let's add the following HTML code to our index.html file.

```
<div class="container">
    This is a container!
</div>
```

Let's then add the following style in styles.css!

```
.container {
    width: 80%;
    height: 300px;
    max-width: 1000px;
```

```
    min-height: 200px;
    background-color: #add8e6;
}
```

Once you save your code and refresh your browser, you can see the requested styles applied to the dimensions. From our code, you can see the big height (300px) and fluid width (80%) amongst other things. You can once again, play around with the styling values to ultimately see the differences.

Fonts

Fonts define the appearance of text.

Fonts in CSS control the appearance of text, allowing you to enhance readability and design. By choosing the right font styles, sizes, and families, you can create visually appealing and professional web pages.

CSS provides the font-family property to specify the typeface, while font-size adjusts how large or small the text appears.

Additional properties like font-weight, font-style, and line-height help refine the look, adding emphasis, boldness, or spacing.

Line-height, which you may not have seen before, is used for line spacing in between each line on your web page!

HTML example (type in index.html):

```
<p id = "bigFont"> This font is HUGE!
</p>

<p class = "text"> Line Height Changes
Spacing! </p>
```

CSS example (type in styles.css):

```
#bigFont {
    font-size: 80px;
    font-weight: bold;
}
.text {
    font-size: 48px;
    line-height: 1.8;
}
```

Refresh your browser to observe these updates!

Tables

Tables organize data into rows and columns.

Tables in HTML are used to organize and display data in a structured format, making it easy to present information like schedules, reports, or pricing plans.

By default, tables consist of rows (<tr>) and columns (<td>), with optional header cells (<th>) for labeling.

CSS enhances tables by allowing you to control their width, height, borders, padding, and spacing, ensuring they align with the overall design of your web page.

With CSS, you can transform basic tables into responsive, visually appealing components that improve user experience and readability.

I am going to take our example from the HTML chapter (Chapter 5) and style it up. Here is the HTML code for reference, type this into index.html:

```
<table>
    <tr>
        <th>State</th>
        <th>Capital</th>
    </tr>
    <tr>
        <td>Texas</td>
        <td>Austin</td>
    </tr>
    <tr>
        <td>Missouri</td>
        <td>Jefferson City</td>
    </tr>
</table>
```

Table CSS Example (type in styles.css):

```css
table {
    width: 100%;
    border-collapse: collapse;
}
th, td {
    border: 1px solid #ddd;
    padding: 10px;
}
th {
    background-color: yellow;
    text-align: left;
}
```

The result should be a table that is evenly spaced out! It should also have a little bit of shading on the first column as well!

Much better than without styling, right?

State	Capital
Texas	Austin
Missouri	Jefferson City

Lists

Lists display items in a structured format. Lists in HTML provide a way to display content in an organized, structured manner. There are three main types of lists: unordered lists (<ul>) for bullet points, ordered lists (<ol>) for numbered items, and definition lists (<dl>) for key-value pairs.

CSS allows you to customize the appearance of lists by modifying the marker styles, spacing, and alignment. For unordered lists, the list-style-type property can change bullets to squares, circles, or even custom images, while ordered lists can use Roman numerals or letters.

Kind of like our table example, I will pull our HTML code from chapter 5 and style it. Take a look at the html below and type it into index.html:

```
<ul>
    <li> Potatoes </li>
    <li> Tomatoes </li>
</ul>


<ol>
    <li> Preheat oven. </li>
    <li> Whip batter. </li>
</ol>
```

Save your code and refresh your browser now to see how it looks!

List CSS Example (type in styles.css):

```
ul {
    list-style-type: square;
}
```

```
li {
    margin: 10px 0;
}
```

This adds a 10 pixel margin to the top and bottom, and a 0px pixel from left to right.

Now, reload your page again. These are pretty minute changes to the previous formatting, so feel free to change them up as you please! Make sure to continuously save and reload your page to see your changes!

Forms

Forms collect user input.

Forms are essential for gathering user input on websites, enabling actions like logging in, signing up, or submitting feedback. In HTML, forms are created using the <form> element, with various input fields such as <input>, <textarea>, <select>, and <button>. Each field can collect different types of data, from text and passwords to checkboxes and file uploads.

A form is always contained between form tags, so write the following:

```
<form></form>
```

Now, let's add 3 questions and a submit button. The first question will ask for the person's name:

```
<label for="name">Name:</label>
<input type="text" id="name"
name="name" placeholder="Enter your
name">
```

Notice how we label the textbox as Name, enter a placeholder, and have an input tag. Let's do the same for a question about their email:

```
<label for="email">Email:</label>
<input type="email" id="email"
name="email" placeholder="Enter your
email">
```

Finally, let's give them a nice textbox for them to enter their message:

```
<label for="message">Message:</label>
<textarea id="message" name="message"
rows="4" placeholder="Enter your
message"></textarea>
```

We specifically use the <textarea> tag for this specific response. Finally, let's add a button with an attribute of submit.

This calls an inbuilt attribute type in HTML to make this a submission button.

```
<button type="submit">Submit</button>
```

CSS enhances forms by improving their layout, styling input fields, and ensuring accessibility. Using properties like width, margin, and padding, you can create clean, organized forms that are easy for users to interact with.

To guide users, CSS can style placeholder text, add focus effects, and display validation messages.

Well-designed forms not only improve aesthetics but also play a critical role in user engagement and data collection.

Refresh our web page to see what this unstyled form looks like.

Now, type in this CSS code to accurately style our form as well:

```
form {
    width: 60%;
    margin: 20px auto;
}
input, textarea {
    width: 100%;
    padding: 10px;
}
```

After refreshing your browser, you should see a pretty professional-looking form, where there are labels, text boxes, and appropriate styling as well!

As of right now, this form is mostly for show - submit does not take any action, but with additional JS knowledge, it can! Now you know how to make the form and get all the components on the page.

Here is a snippet of all my code and the resulting web page!

```html
<!DOCTYPE html>
<html lang="en">
<head>
    <meta charset="UTF-8">
    <meta name="viewport" content="width=device-width, initial-scale=1.0">
    <title>Document</title>
    <link rel="stylesheet" href="styles.css">

</head>
<body>

    <h1> Welcome to my CSS Website! </h1>

    <p class="intro">Let's learn CSS!</p>

    <p id="welcome">Here, we use an ID to style text!</p>

    <h1>CSS Colors</h1>
    <p>CSS lets you apply vibrant colors to web elements.</p>
    <p class="highlight">This paragraph has a highlighted background.</p>
```

```html
22    <div class="box">
23        This box has a dashed green border.
24    </div>
25
26    <div class="container">
27        This is a container!
28    </div>
29
30    <p id = "bigFont">This font is HUGE!</p>
31
32    <p class = "text"> Line Height Changes Spacing! </p>
33
34    <table>
35        <tr>
36            <th>State</th>
37            <th>Capital</th>
38        </tr>
39        <tr>
40
41            <td>Texas</td>
42            <td>Austin</td>
43        </tr>
44        <tr>
45            <td>Missouri</td>
46            <td>Jefferson City</td>
47        </tr>
48        </table>
49
50
51    <ul>
52        <li> Potatoes </li>
53        <li> Tomatoes </li>
54    </ul>
55
56    <ol>
57        <li> Preheat oven. </li>
58
59        <li> Whip batter. </li>
60    </ol>
61
62    <form>
63        <label for="name">Name:</label>
64        <input type="text" id="name" name="name" placeholder="Enter your name">
65
66        <label for="email">Email:</label>
67        <input type="email" id="email" name="email" placeholder="Enter your email">
68
69        <label for="message">Message:</label>
70        <textarea id="message" name="message" rows="4" placeholder="Enter your message"></textarea>
71
72        <button type="submit">Submit</button>
73    </form>
74
75
76 </body>
77 </html>
```

```css
 1  h1
 2  {
 3      text-align: center;
 4      color: ■#ff6347;
 5  }
 6
 7
 8  .intro
 9  {
10      text-align: right;
11      font-size: 20px;
12  }
13
14  #welcome
15  {
16      color: ■blue;
17      font-size: 60px;
18  }
19
20  body
21  {
22      background-color: □#f0f8ff;
23  }
24
25  p
26  {
27      color: ■rgb(50, 50, 50);
28  }
29
30  .highlight {
31      background-color: □yellow;
32      color: ■black;
33  }
34
35  .box {
36      border: 3px dashed ■#4caf50;
37      padding: 10px;
38      width: 50%;
39      margin: 20px;
40      background-color: □#fff3cd;
41  }
```

```css
43  .container {
44      width: 80%;
45      height: 300px;
46      max-width: 1000px;
47      min-height: 200px;
48      background-color: ☐#add8e6;
49  }
50
51  #bigFont {
52      font-size: 80px;
53      font-weight: bold;
54  }
55  .text {
56      font-size: 48px;
57      line-height: 1.8;
58  }
59
60  table {
61      width: 100%;
62      border-collapse: collapse;
63  }
64
65  th, td {
66      border: 1px solid ☐#ddd;
67      padding: 10px;
68  }
69
70  th {
71      background-color: ☐yellow;
72      text-align: left;
73  }
74
75  ul {
76      list-style-type: square;
77  }
78
79  li {
80      margin: 10px 0;
81  }
82
83  form {
84      width: 60%;
```

```
85        margin: 20px auto;
86  }
87
88  input, textarea {
89      width: 100%;
90      padding: 10px;
91  }
```

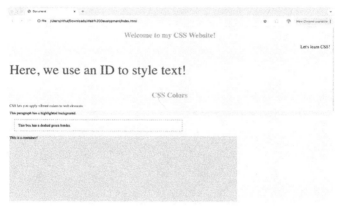

This font is HUGE!

Line Height Changes Spacing!

Check For Understanding

1. Which CSS property changes text color?

2. How do you target an HTML element with class="button"?

3. What does margin: 10px; mean?

4. What's the difference between padding and margin?

5. How do you make text bold in CSS?

Check For Understanding (Answers)

1. color (e.g., color: blue;)

2. .button { ... } (dot prefix for classes)

3. 10px margins around the specified element

4. Padding = space *inside* an element; Margin = space *outside*

5. font-weight: bold; or <strong> tag

Chapter 8: CSS Tools/Libraries

What is Bootstrap?

Bootstrap is one of the most popular CSS frameworks used to create modern, responsive, and visually appealing websites quickly and easily. It is a library of pre-written CSS and JavaScript code that you can plug into your own project to save time and avoid writing everything from scratch.

Instead of writing complex CSS to handle layouts, buttons, navigation bars, forms, and other components, Bootstrap gives you ready-to-use classes that do all the heavy lifting. By simply adding these classes to your HTML elements, you can create professional-looking designs without needing to write a lot of custom CSS.

To use Bootstrap, you simply need to link to its stylesheet and JavaScript files. The easiest way is by using a CDN (Content Delivery Network), which allows you to load Bootstrap files directly from the internet.

Search "bootstrap css" online to learn more about the documentation. Take a look at a simple example of bootstrap in action once you've done all the groundwork.

```
<!DOCTYPE html>
<html lang="en">
<head>
  <meta charset="UTF-8">
  <meta name="viewport" content="width=device-width, initial-scale=1.0">
  <title>Simple Bootstrap Button</title>
  <!-- Bootstrap CSS -->
  <link href="https://cdn.jsdelivr.net/npm/bootstrap@5.1.3/dist/css/boots
</head>
<body>
  <!-- Simple Button -->
  <button>Normal button</button>
  <button class="btn btn-primary">Bootstrap button</button>

  <!-- Bootstrap JS (Optional) -->
  <script src="https://cdn.jsdelivr.net/npm/bootstrap@5.1.3/dist/js/boots
</body>
</html>
```

Look at the automatic difference from the normal to the bootstrap button! Bootstrap gave us a predefined class to apply, and it did the styling for us. Very helpful!

Uses of Bootstrap

Bootstrap is a powerful tool that can be used for many purposes. Here are some of the key things you can do with Bootstrap:

Responsive Design:

Bootstrap makes your website automatically adjust to different screen sizes — desktops, tablets, and phones. You don't need to write complicated CSS media queries; Bootstrap's grid system handles this for you!

Pre-styled Components:

Bootstrap gives you buttons, forms, navbars, cards, modals, and more — all already styled and ready to use.

Mobile-Friendly Navigation Bars:

You can easily create responsive navigation bars that collapse into menus on smaller screens. No need to write JavaScript for this; Bootstrap does it all.

Consistent Design:

Using Bootstrap ensures that all parts of your website have a consistent look and feel. You don't need to worry about manually adjusting margins, padding, or colors — Bootstrap keeps it neat.

Fast Prototyping:

If you want to create a prototype or demo of your website quickly, Bootstrap is the perfect tool. With minimal effort, you can have a fully working layout and design.

Accessibility:

Bootstrap's components are built to be accessible by default, which helps ensure that people using screen readers and other assistive technology can still interact with your site.

Check For Understanding

1. What is Bootstrap?

2. How do you add Bootstrap to your HTML file?

3. Name two types of elements or components you can create using Bootstrap.

4. How does Bootstrap help with responsive design?

5. Why might someone prefer to use Bootstrap instead of writing all CSS from scratch?

Check For Understanding Answers

1. Bootstrap is a CSS framework that provides pre-written CSS and JavaScript code to create responsive and styled websites easily.
2. You can add Bootstrap to your HTML file by linking to its CDN in the <head> section using the provided <link> and <script> tags.
3. Buttons, navigation bars, forms, cards, modals, and more.
4. Bootstrap uses a grid system and responsive classes that automatically adjust the layout of your website to different screen sizes like mobile, tablet, and desktop.
5. Because Bootstrap saves time by offering ready-to-use components, ensures consistent design, and simplifies responsive web design without writing complex CSS.

Chapter 9: JavaScript Overview

What is JavaScript?

JavaScript (JS) is a lightweight, interpreted language that runs in the browser. It enables developers to manipulate web elements, respond to user input, and communicate with servers. It was initially designed to make web pages interactive, but it has since evolved into a full-fledged programming language used for both front-end and back-end development.

Where is JavaScript Used?

Web development: Creating interactive user interfaces, dynamic forms, and real-time content updates.

Game development: Used with HTML5 Canvas for creating browser-based games.

Server-side programming: Node.js allows JavaScript to run on the server, handling databases and APIs.

Mobile applications: Frameworks like React Native enable mobile app development using JavaScript.

Machine learning: Libraries like TensorFlow.js bring AI capabilities to JavaScript.

First JavaScript Program

Since we are starting off with simpler scripting, we are going to write all our JS (JavaScript) internally, or within the HTML file, for this book.

Let's start off by creating a new HTML file for this section, and let's name it **enhancedHTML.html**. Type in the ! and get the default page ready.

Now, let's add a default button that we learned in Chapter 5 (Elements & Attributes). Your code should look something like this:

```
<> enhancedHTML.html > ⊘ html > ⊘ body > ⊘ button
1    <!DOCTYPE html>
2    <html lang="en">
3    <head>
4        <meta charset="UTF-8">
5        <meta name="viewport" content="width=device-width, initial-scale=1.0">
6        <title>Document</title>
7    </head>
8    <body>
9        <button>Click Me</button>
10   </body>
11   </html>
```

Now, let's add the following code within the button tag to make it interactive with HTML:

```
<button onclick="alert('Hello,
JavaScript!')">Click Me</button>
```

Go to your file explorer and open the file in your browser! See what it does! On the button click, it pops up a dialog window that says "Hello, JavaScript!" This is one of the ways that JS can pair with HTML, but it's better to learn it after knowing a few JavaScript basics.

The Script Tag

The JS that we just wrote happened to be within the HTML element itself, because we wrote the portion of JS code literally inside the button tag. However, usually, when JavaScript is written in HTML, it will be written within the script tag, much like how most of our HTML code was within the body tag:

```
<script> </script>
```

The script tag is located at the bottom of our body tag. It is still in the body tag, but after all our HTML code. Let's add our script tag to the enhancedHTML.html file.

Console.log()

Before jumping into JS concepts, let's test out our script tag and see how it works without our debugging console. To do this, we can use the console.log() method, which prints our JavaScript content to our debugging console.

Add the following code in our script tag:

```
console.log("Cool! It prints in console!");
```

Even though we have written our code, we have to run it differently than we have with our HTML and CSS previously. Please read the next section to learn how to run the above code!

READ CAREFULLY: Let's see how to run this JS program in order to see our output properly.

1. Go to the top menu of VSCode and click on the "View" tab
2. Now, click the option that says "Debug Console". This is where we will see the output of our program.

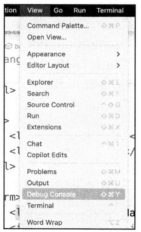

3. Go to the top menu again and select the "Run" tab.
4. Click on "Run Without Debugging." Click your browser of choice as you did this entire book. This will run your program. Keep in mind you have to navigate back to the "debug console" after you run, even when the web page pops up.

You should see the following output in your Debug Console (near the bottom of your IDE screen):

READ CAREFULLY: After running your program once, you must terminate (end) the program either by closing out of the web page or clicking the stop button at the top of VSCode.

JavaScript Basics

Now, we will go over a bunch of JavaScript basics that I highly recommend you type in and test within VSCode.

Variables and Data Types:

In JavaScript, variables are used to store data values. They act as containers for information that can be referenced and manipulated in your code. JavaScript uses var, let, and const to declare variables. They follow this syntax:

```
[type of variable] [name of variable] =
[value];
```

With this knowledge, let's make the following 3 variables. Type this in the <script> tag of enhancedHTML.html.

```
let name = "Tom Cruise";
const coolnessRating = 9;
var isCool = true;
```

We made 3 types of variables here. First, we let a string (text) named "name" be assigned a value of "Tom Cruise." The second variable was a constant named coolnessRating, which he gets a 9 for. Last, we had a variable called isCool, which is a Boolean value (true or false). We set that to true, because Tom Cruise is one of the coolest actors ever.

If we run our code now, we will not see anything as we only created variables. Let's use the console.log() method to print these to the terminal:

```
console.log(name);
console.log(coolnessRating);
console.log(isCool);
```

Remember, you run your program by clicking Run -> Run without Debugging in the top navigation bar.

REMINDER: After running your program once, you must terminate (end) the program either by closing out of the web page or clicking the stop button at the top of VSCode. After terminating, run your program again to see changes!

Now, we should see the following in our console like so.

```
∨ enhancedHTML.html ×

∨ enhancedHTML.html  ⟩ ⟨⟩ html  ⟩ ⟨⟩ body  ⟩ ⟨⟩ script
  1  <!DOCTYPE html>
  2  <html lang="en">
  3  <head>
  4      <meta charset="UTF-8">
  5      <meta name="viewport" content="width=device-width, initial-scale=1.0">
  6      <title>Document</title>
  7  </head>
  8  <body>
  9      <button onclick="alert('Hello, JavaScript!')">Click Me</button>
 10
 11      <script>
 12          console.log("Cool! It prints in console!");
 13
 14          let name = "Tom Cruise";
 15          const coolnessRating = 9;
 16          var isCool = true;
 17
 18
 19          console.log(name);
 20          console.log(coolnessRating);
 21          console.log(isCool);
```

Functions:

We've spent a bunch of time writing new code, but what if you want to reuse some of it? Functions allow you to reuse code efficiently. You can call these again and again when you want to replicate the same functionality:

Function writing syntax:

```
function functionName() {
    // Code to execute
}
```

Function calling syntax:

```
functionName();
```

We can also use something called parameters, which pass variables into the function:

Function with parameter syntax:

```
function functionName(parameterName) {
    // Code to execute
}
```

Calling function with parameter syntax:

```
functionName(variableName);
```

Example (type in enhancedHTML.html within <script> tag):

```
function greet(user) {
    return "Hello, " + user;
}
console.log(greet("Spiderman"));
```

When you run: The output will be "Hello, Spiderman". Let's break down how this code works. First, we create a function named greet, and it takes a parameter of user.

A parameter is just a temporary variable that you can use within your function, ours is named user! The return statement is what our function will output after running, so we will output "Hello, [user]".

When we call the function by saying greet("Spiderman"), we are telling the function what the value of our user variable is, so that when it wants to output the result, we get "Hello, Spiderman" in our terminal!

Conditional Statements:

Conditional statements control the flow of your program by executing different blocks of code based on whether a condition is true or false. The most common conditional is the if...else statement.

Syntax:

```
if ([condition]) {
    [code to run if true]
} else {
    [code to run if false]
}
```

Example (type in enhancedHTML.html within <script> tag):

```
let num = 10;
if (num > 5) {
    console.log("Number is greater than 5");
```

```
} else {
    console.log("Number is 5 or less");
}
```

When you run the code, it should say:
```
Number is greater than 5
```

Run it in your console and take a look!

The condition num > 5 checks if 10 is greater than 5 (which is true).

Since the condition passes, the if block runs, printing "Number is greater than 5".

If num were 4, the else block would run instead, printing "Number is 5 or less".

Loops:

Loops allow you to execute a block of code multiple times. This is useful when you want to repeat an action without writing the same code over and over again. We are going to be learning about for loops.

Let's take a look at the syntax for it:

```
for ([initialization]; [condition];
[increment/decrement]) {
```

```
    [loop body]
}
```

That seems pretty confusing, so let's type up the example in enhancedHTML.html within <script> tag and then analyze it:

```
for (let i = 1; i <= 5; i++) {
    console.log("Counting: " + i);
}
```

When you run: The console will print:

```
Counting 1
Counting 2
Counting 3
Counting 4
Counting 5
```

Let's break down how this works:

Initialization (let i = 1) – We start by declaring a variable i and setting it to 1. This variable will keep track of how many times the loop has run.

Condition (i <= 5) – Before each iteration, the loop checks if i is still less than or equal to 5. If true, the loop continues; if false, it stops.

Increment (i++) – After each iteration, i increases by 1.
This ensures the loop progresses and eventually exits when
i reaches anything above 5.

Loop Body (console.log(...)) – This is the code that runs in
every iteration, printing the current value of i.

This loop runs 5 times, printing each iteration until i is no
longer less than or equal to 5.

Arrays:

Arrays allow you to store multiple values in a single
variable, making it easier to manage collections of data.

Syntax:

```
let [arrayName] = [value1, value2,
...];
```

Example (type in enhancedHTML.html within <script>
tag):

```
let fruits = ["Apple", "Banana",
"Cherry"];
console.log(fruits[1]);
```

When you run: We will see "banana" in the console.

Let's break it down:

Arrays are zero-indexed, meaning the first element is at position 0, the second at 1, and so on.

Here, fruits[1] access the second element ("Banana").

If we used fruits[0], it would return "Apple".

Arrays are useful when you need an ordered list of items, like a shopping list or a series of names.

Take a look at the final code snippet for reference!

```
enhancedHTML.html ×
enhancedHTML.html > html > body > script
1   <!DOCTYPE html>
2   <html lang="en">
3   <head>
4       <meta charset="UTF-8">
5       <meta name="viewport" content="width=device-width, initial-scale=1.0">
6       <title>Document</title>
7   </head>
8   <body>
9       <button onclick="alert('Hello, JavaScript!')">Click Me</button>
10
11      <script>
12          console.log("Cool! It prints in console!");
13
14          let name = "Tom Cruise";
15          const coolnessRating = 9;
16          var isCool = true;
17
18
19          console.log(name);
20          console.log(coolnessRating);
21          console.log(isCool);
```

```
22
23
24          function greet(user) {
25              return 'Hello, " + user;
26          }
27          console.log(greet("Spiderman"));
28
29          let num = 13;
30          if (num > 5) {
31              console.log("Number is greater than 5");
32          } else {
33              console.log("Number is 5 or less");
34          }
35
36          for (let i = 1; i <= 5; i++) {
37              console.log("Counting: " + i);
38          }
39
40
41          let fruits = ["Apple", "Banana", "Cherry"];
42          console.log(fruits[1]);
43
44
45      </script>
46  </body>
47  </html>
```

PROBLEMS   OUTPUT   **DEBUG CONSOLE**   TERMINAL   · · ·   Filter (e.g. text, !exclude, \escape)

```
Cool! It prints in console!
Tom Cruise
9
true
Hello, Spiderman
Number is greater than 5
Counting: 1
Counting: 2
Counting: 3
Counting: 4
Counting: 5
Banana
```

Check for Understanding

1. What is the difference between let, const, and var?

2. How does JavaScript interact with HTML elements?

3. Write a function that takes a number as input and returns its square.

4. Write a function that logs "Hello, World!" to the console.

Check for Understanding Answers

1. var is function-scoped and can be redeclared.

   let is block-scoped and cannot be redeclared within the same scope.

   const is block-scoped, must be assigned a value upon declaration, and cannot be reassigned.

2. JavaScript interacts with HTML via the DOM (Document Object Model) using methods like document.getElementById() and event listeners to modify elements dynamically.

3.
```
function square(num) {

     return num * num;
}
console.log(square(4));
```

4.
```
function sayHello() {

   console.log("Hello, World!");
}

sayHello();
```

Chapter 10: JavaScript Uses with HTML/CSS

Now that you know the basics of JavaScript, let's marry those skills with HTML. Begin by creating interact.html.

As usual, let's set it up with the "!"

Make sure to add the <script> tag as well.

PLEASE READ: The "Run Without Debugging" method for the last chapter does not carry over here. From now on, run your program by going back to your file and opening it through a web browser, and then refreshing your browser to see changes!

Variables

We can use our previous knowledge of variables from the last chapter to print it on our web page. Type the following (in the <script> tag):

```
let message = "Welcome to JavaScript!";
alert(message);
```

Here, we declare a variable message and assign it the string "Welcome to JavaScript!". The alert() function is used to display a pop-up with the value of the variable.

Go to your files and open this file in your browser! You should see the popup message right when you load the page.

You can alter and manipulate these variables in other ways as well - this alert is the tip of the iceberg!

Functions

To carry out reusable functionality within our program, we can use functions. You "call" functions throughout your program, and they will do the task that you programmed them to.

We developed a greet() function last chapter, and I am writing a similar function now. Write the following in the script tag of interact.html:

```
function greetUser(name) {

  alert("Hello, " + name + "!");
}
greetUser("Batman");
```

Here, We define a function greetUser() that takes a parameter (name) and displays a greeting message using that parameter.

The greetUser("Batman") call runs the function, and the alert will display "Hello, Batman!".

Run/Refresh your page! When the page loads, an alert will appear with the message "Hello, Batman!".

Interacting with HTML with IDs

One of the best things about JS in HTML is that it can call functions on the web page. Additionally, we can tie this result to certain elements on our screen. Let's start off by adding a simple button to our HTML, and making it identifiable with an ID:

```
<button id="myButton">Click me</button>
```

Refresh your browser - nothing happens! However, we can use an awesome function called getElementByID that will tie together elements of HTML with functionality from JS!

Look at this syntax:

```
document.getElementById("elementId")
[any other specification]
```

Now, type in the following JS code (in the <script> tag) that will send an alert every time the button is clicked:

```
document.getElementById("myButton").onc
lick = function() {
    alert("Hello, you clicked the
button!");
};
```

We can also change text and manipulate HTML elements with the same function: getElementById!

Let's make this change happen on the click of a button by adding this code to a function and then calling it!

Example (type in the <body> tag in interact.html):

```
<p id="welcome">Original Text</p>
<button onclick="changeText()">Change
Text</button>
```

Example (type in your <script> tag in interact.html):

```
function changeText() {
document.getElementById("welcome").inne
rHTML = "Text Modified";
}
```

In our code, we have a button that calls the changeText function. This function is defined in our JS, where we change the text to "Text Modified". Refresh your webpage!

After clicking the "change text" button, it should look like this:

You can tinker around with other "getElementById" operations in your own time as well!

Here is the final code for this file and the following web page outputs as well!

```html
interact.html ×
interact.html > html > body > script
1   <!DOCTYPE html>
2   <html lang="en">
3   <head>
4       <meta charset="UTF-8">
5       <meta name="viewport" content="width=device-width, initial-scale=1.0">
6       <title>Document</title>
7   </head>
8   <body>
9
10
11      <button id="myButton">Click me</button>
12      <p id="welcome">Original Text</p>
13      <button onclick="changeText()">Change Text</button>
14
15      <script>
16
17          let message = "Welcome to JavaScript!";
18          alert(message);
19
20          function greetUser(name) {
21              alert("Hello, " + name + "!");
22          }
23          greetUser("Batman");
24
25          document.getElementById("myButton").onclick = function() {
26              alert("Hello, you clicked the button!");
27          };
28          function changeText() {
29              document.getElementById("welcome").innerHTML = "Text Modified";
30          }
31
32
33      </script>
34  </body>
35  </html>
```

Check for Understanding

1. How do you select an HTML element with id="title" in CSS?

2. What JavaScript method grabs an element by its ID for styling?

3. How do you link a CSS file to an HTML document?

4. What's the difference between .class and #id selectors?

Check for Understanding Answers

1. CSS ID selector: #title { ... }

2. DOM access: document.getElementById("title")

3. Linking CSS: <link rel="stylesheet"

   href="styles.css"> within <head> tag

4. Selector difference:

   a. .class → reusable (many elements)

   b. #id → unique (single element)

Chapter 11: Let's Make a Website!

We have learned so many different HTML, CSS, and JavaScript concepts throughout this book. Now, it's time to put it all together and create a mini-website!

Before we can code anything, however, let's set up the pages and files that we will need. Let's make a 3-page company website with a CSS file, and create the following files:

1. home.html
2. aboutus.html
3. contact.html
4. styleWebsite.css

Home.html

Let's start off with our homepage. Everything in this subsection should be written in home.html. We will keep this simple, but still neat and nice. Type in "!" and hit enter to start up our default layout.

Now, let's build our page from the top! Our first step will be adding a navigation bar.

Next, let's add our stylesheet, styleWebsite.css, by adding the following code in our <head> tag:

```
<link rel="stylesheet"
href="styleWebsite.css">
```

Navigation Bar

Navigation bars create menus for websites. I'll give you the HTML for this. Place at the top of the <body> tag in home.html.

```
<nav>
  <a href="home.html">Home</a>
  <a href="aboutus.html">About Us</a>
  <a href="contact.html">Contact</a>
<nav>
```

A navigation bar is a key component of any website, providing users with an intuitive way to move between different pages or sections. In HTML, navigation bars are typically created using the <nav> element, which can contain lists (<ul>) of links (<a>).

Notice how our HTML code is just a nav "list" tag with a bunch of links.

CSS is important in styling this list into a nice menu for users.

Add the following CSS code to style our navbar in styleWebsite.css:

```
nav {
    background-color: #2c3e50;
    padding: 15px 0;
    text-align: center;
```

```
    box-shadow: 0 2px 5px rgba(0,0,0,0.1);
}



nav a {
    color: white;
    text-decoration: none;
    margin: 0 15px;
    padding: 5px 10px;
    font-size: 18px;
    transition: all 0.3s ease;
}
```

"nav" is just selecting all navbar tags. "nav a" selects the
<a> tags of every tag named nav!

Now, you should see a nice dark navbar at the top of the
screen. It should also link to the other pages now too, but
they are all blank.

**READ CAREFULLY: Let's copy this exact code
(ctrl+a) and paste it in aboutus.html and contact.html.
Now, we will have the navbar accessible in each of our
pages!**

Great! Our linkage is all set up! Let's put some content on our page now.

For the sake of making a web page, I will only cover the surface of each of these web pages. In fact, I may only put a few lines of code for each page, so that you can tinker around with it and make it your own!

I want to make a website a fictional company.

Now, I will just add the following header in home.html:

```
<h1 id="mainMessage"> Welcome to my
company! Click on the other tabs to
explore! </h1>
```

And style it up (I added a bunch of stuff in styleWebsite, you can choose what you'd like):

```
#mainMessage {
    font-family: 'Montserrat', 'Arial',
sans-serif;
    font-size: 3.5rem;
    font-weight: 700;
    color: white;
    text-align: center;
    margin: 1.5rem 0;
    padding: 1rem;
}
```

Home.html is done for instruction - you can add additional elements and style them as you wish.

AboutUs.html

Now, let's add an information section about our company. Here is what my <body> tag for AboutUs.html looks like:

```
<nav>
   <a href="home.html">Home</a>
   <a href="aboutus.html">About Us</a>
   <a href="contact.html">Contact</a>
  <nav>

  <div class="container">
    <section class="about-section">
      <div class="about-content">
        <div class="about-text">

           <h1>About Rithul's LEGO Store</h1>
           <p>Mission Statement</p>

           <h2>Our Brick-tastic Story</h2>
           <p>Story Info</p>

           <h2>What We Build</h2>
           <p>Building Info</p>

        </div>
      </div>
    </section>
  </div>
```

Add this css to styleWebsite.css:

```css
* {
    margin: 0;
    padding: 0;
    box-sizing: border-box;
    font-family: 'Arial', sans-serif;
}

body {
    background-color: #f8f9fa;
    color: #333;
    line-height: 1.6;
}

.container {
    max-width: 1200px;
    margin: 0 auto;
    padding: 20px;
}
.about-section {
    padding: 80px 0;
    background-color: #fff;
    border-radius: 8px;
    box-shadow: 0 4px 12px rgba(0, 0, 0, 0.1);
    margin: 40px 0;
}

.about-content {
    display: flex;
    flex-wrap: wrap;
    align-items: center;
    justify-content: space-between;
}
```

```css
.about-text {
    flex: 1;
    min-width: 300px;
    padding: 0 40px;
}
```

Contact.html

Finally, let's give our users a way to contact us and build a form. For simplicity, I will just use the same form we created earlier in the book:

HTML Code:

```html
<form>
      <label for="name">Name:</label>
      <input type="text" id="name" name="name"
placeholder="Enter your name">

      <label for="email">Email:</label>
      <input type="email" id="email" name="email"
placeholder="Enter your email">

      <label for="message">Message:</label>
      <textarea id="message" name="message"
rows="4" placeholder="Enter your
message"></textarea>

      <button type="submit">Submit</button>
</form>
```

CSS Code:

```css
h1 {
    font-size: 2.5rem;
    margin-bottom: 20px;
    color: #2c3e50;
}

h2 {
    font-size: 1.8rem;
    margin: 30px 0 15px;
    color: #3498db;
}

p {
    margin-bottom: 15px;
    font-size: 1.1rem;
}

form {
    width: 60%;
    margin: 20px auto;
}

input, textarea {
    width: 100%;
    padding: 10px;
}
```

The form currently cannot perform functionality, but with JavaScript you can make it do so! Additionally JS knowledge can help to even greater things, but that goes beyond this book.

Yay! We finished our simple 3-page website with HTML and CSS! Here are my final code snippets and the website pages themselves! Make sure to save all your files and then launch home.html to view the website!

Home.html:

```
home.html ×      aboutus.html      contact.html      # styleWebsite.css                                    ⊡ ▾
home.html  62 kb
 1   <!DOCTYPE html>
 2   <html lang="en">
 3   <head>
 4       <meta charset="UTF-8">
 5       <meta name="viewport" content="width=device-width, initial-scale=1.0">
 6       <title>My First Website</title>
 7       <link rel="stylesheet" href="styleWebsite.css">
 8   </head>
 9   <body>
10       <nav>
11           <a href="home.html">Home</a>
12           <a href="aboutus.html">About Us</a>
13           <a href="contact.html">Contact</a>
14       <nav>
15
16       <h1 id="mainMessage"> Welcome to my website! Click on the other tabs to explore! </h1>
17
18
19   </body>
20   </html>
```

AboutUs.html:

```
<!DOCTYPE html>
<html lang="en">
<head>
    <meta charset="UTF-8">
    <meta name="viewport" content="width=device-width, initial-scale=1.0">
    <title>My First Website</title>
    <link rel="stylesheet" href="styleWebsite.css">
</head>
<body>
    <nav>
        <a href="home.html">Home</a>
        <a href="aboutus.html">About Us</a>
        <a href="contact.html">Contact</a>
    <nav>

    <div class="container">
        <section class="about-section">
            <div class="about-content">
                <div class="about-text">
                    <h1>About Rithul's LEGO Store</h1>
                    <p>Mission Statement</p>


                    <h2>Our Brick-tastic Story</h2>
                    <p>Story Info</p>

                    <h2>What We Build</h2>
                    <p>Building Info</p>
                </div>
            </div>
        </section>
    </div>
</body>
</html>
```

Contact.html:

```html
<!DOCTYPE html>
<html lang="en">
<head>
    <meta charset="UTF-8">
    <meta name="viewport" content="width=device-width, initial-scale=1.0">
    <title>My First Website</title>
    <link rel="stylesheet" href="styleWebsite.css">
</head>
<body>
    <nav>
        <a href="home.html">Home</a>
        <a href="aboutus.html">About Us</a>
        <a href="contact.html">Contact</a>
    <nav>

    <form>
        <label for="name">Name:</label>
        <input type="text" id="name" name="name" placeholder="Enter your name">

        <label for="email">Email:</label>
        <input type="email" id="email" name="email" placeholder="Enter your email">

        <label for="message">Message:</label>
        <textarea id="message" name="message" rows="4" placeholder="Enter your message"></textarea>

        <button type="submit">Submit</button>

    </form>

</body>
</html>
```

styleWebsite.css:

```css
1   /* Navigation Bar Styles */
2   nav {
3       background-color: #2c3e50;
4       padding: 15px 0;
5       text-align: center;
6       box-shadow: 0 2px 5px rgba(0,0,0,0.1);
7   }
8
9   nav a {
10      color: white;
11      text-decoration: none;
12      margin: 0 15px;
13      padding: 5px 10px;
14      font-size: 18px;
15      transition: all 0.3s ease;
16  }
17
18  nav a:hover {
19      color: #3498db;
20      background-color: rgba(255,255,255,0.1);
21      border-radius: 4px;
22  }
23
24  #mainMessage {
25      font-family: 'Montserrat', 'Arial', sans-serif; /* Modern, clean font */
26      font-size: 3.5rem; /* Large, attention-grabbing size */

27      font-weight: 700; /* Bold weight for impact */
28      color: white; /* Sophisticated dark gray */
29      text-align: center; /* Perfectly centered */
30      margin: 1.5rem 0; /* Balanced spacing */
31      padding: 1rem; /* Comfortable padding */
32  }
33
34  /* Global Styles */
35  * {
36      margin: 0;
37      padding: 0;
38      box-sizing: border-box;
39      font-family: 'Arial', sans-serif;
40  }
41
42  body {
43      background-color: #f8f9fa;
44      color: #333;
45      line-height: 1.6;
46  }
47
48  .container {
49      max-width: 1200px;
50      margin: 0 auto;
51      padding: 20px;
```

132

```css
52  }
53
54  /* About Us Section */
55  .about-section {
56      padding: 80px 0;
57      background-color: □#fff;
58      border-radius: 8px;
59      box-shadow: 0 4px 12px □rgba(0, 0, 0, 0.1);
60      margin: 40px 0;
61  }
62
63  .about-content {
64      display: flex;
65      flex-wrap: wrap;
66      align-items: center;
67      justify-content: space-between;
68  }
69
70  .about-text {
71      flex: 1;
72      min-width: 300px;
73      padding: 0 40px;
74  }
75
76  .about-image {
77      flex: 1;
78      min-width: 300px;
79      text-align: center;
80      padding: 20px;
81  }
82
83  .about-image img {
84      max-width: 100%;
85      border-radius: 8px;
86      box-shadow: 0 4px 8px □rgba(0, 0, 0, 0.1);
87  }
88
89  h1 {
90      font-size: 2.5rem;
91      margin-bottom: 20px;
92      color: ■#2c3e50;
93  }
94
95  h2 {
96      font-size: 1.8rem;
97      margin: 30px 0 15px;
98      color: □#3498db;
99  }
100
101 p {
102     margin-bottom: 15px;
103     font-size: 1.1rem;
104 }
105
106 form {
107     width: 60%;
108     margin: 20px auto;
109 }
110
111 input, textarea {
112     width: 100%;
113     padding: 10px;
114 }
```

133

Home.html (Page):

AboutUs.html (Page):

Contact.html (Page):

Glossary:

HTML Terms:

Anchor (<a>) – Creates hyperlinks.

Attribute – Extra information within a tag (e.g., href).

Body (<body>) – Contains visible web page content.

Button (<button>) – Clickable button.

Div (<div>) – Block-level container.

DOCTYPE – Declares the HTML version (<!DOCTYPE html>).

Element – A component of an HTML document (e.g., <p>).

Form (<form>) – Collects user input.

Head (<head>) – Contains meta-information.

HTML – HyperText Markup Language.

Image (<img>) – Embeds an image.

Input (<input>) – User input field.

Link (<link>) – Connects external resources (e.g., CSS).

List – Ordered (<ol>) or unordered (<ul>).

Meta Tag (<meta>) – Provides metadata.

Table (<table>) – Displays tabular data.

Tag – Markers that define elements (e.g., <h1>).

CSS Terms (Alphabetical Order)

Border – Edge around an element.

Box Model – Content, padding, border, margin.

Class (.class) – Reusable style.

Display – Controls layout (block, flex).

Flexbox – Flexible layout model.

Float – Wraps text around elements.

Grid – Two-dimensional layout system.

ID (#id) – Unique identifier.

Margin – Space outside an element.

Padding – Space inside an element.

Property – Defines style (color, font-size).

Selector – Targets HTML elements (h1, .class).

Specificity – Determines which styles apply.

Value – Specifies property settings (red, 16px).

Variable (Custom Property, --var) – Reusable values.

JavaScript Terms:

API – Application Programming Interface.

Array ([1, 2, 3]) – Ordered list.

Boolean – true or false.

Callback – Function passed as an argument.

ClassList – Modifies CSS classes.

Conditional (if, else) – Decision-making.

Console (console.log) – Displays JS logs.

Data Type – String, Number, Boolean, etc.

DOM – Document Object Model (HTML as objects).

DOM Manipulation – Changing HTML/CSS via JS.

Function – Reusable code block.

Get Element By ID (getElementById) – Selects by ID.

JavaScript (JS) – Adds interactivity to web pages.

Loop (for, while) – Repeats code.

Number – Numeric value (42).

Parameter – Function input.

Return – Outputs a value from a function.

Scope – Variable accessibility.

String ("Hello") – Text.

Variable (let, const, var) – Stores data.

Closing Remarks

Thank you for making it to the end of the book. Whether you bought this book online, borrowed it from the library, or acquired it in a different manner, I truly appreciate you taking the time to go through it all. If you have not read *A High Schooler's Guide to Java*, I highly recommend it as well!

Continue to tinker around with languages, web development, and more! See what you can create with your code! Increase what you know and use it in your programming!

Thank you again,

- Rithul Bhat

www.ingramcontent.com/pod-product-compliance
Lightning Source LLC
LaVergne TN
LVHW022323060326
832902LV00020B/3634